Loving Thoughts
for Tender Hearts

A Special Gift

To

_____

From

_____

Date

_____

Loving Thoughts
for Tender Hearts

Edited by Paul C. Brownlow

Brownlow Publishing Company, Inc.

Ribbons of Love

GARDENS OF FRIENDSHIP

HAPPY IS THE HOUSE
That Shelters a Friend

IN THE PRESENCE OF ANGELS

JUST FOR YOU:
A Celebration of Joy and Friendship

LOVING THOUGHTS
for Tender Hearts

MOTHER
Another Word for Love

Table of Contents

CHAPTER ONE
Never Too Much

Love is the one ingredient of which our world never tires and of which there is never an abundance. It is needed in the market-place and in the mansions. It is needed in the ghettos and in the governments. It is needed in homes, in hospitals, and in individual hearts. The world will never outgrow its need for love.

C. NEIL STRAIT

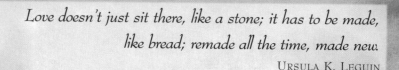

Love doesn't just sit there, like a stone; it has to be made,
like bread; remade all the time, made new.

Ursula K. Leguin

Outwitted

He drew a circle that shut me out
Heretic, rebel, a thing to flout.
But love and I had the wit to win:
We drew a circle that took him in.

Edwin Markham

All one can do is leave open a window so the breeze of love…
may come in. If a window is open, the breeze may still
not blow in; there is no guarantee. There is, however,
one guarantee: if the window is not open,
the breeze will not blow in.

JOEL KRAMER

In comparison with a loving human being,
everything else is worthless.

HUGH MACLENNAN

I Love You

I love you not only for what you are, but for what I am when I am with you. I love you not only for what you have made of yourself, but for what you are making of me. I love you for the part of me that you bring out. I love you for putting your hand into my heaped-up heart, and passing over all the foolish and frivolous and weak things which you cannot help dimly seeing there, and for drawing out into the light all the beautiful, radiant belongings, that no one else had looked quite far enough to find.

I love you for ignoring the possibilities of the fool and weakling in me, and for laying firm hold on the possibilities of good in me. I love you for closing your eyes to the discords in me, and for adding to the music in me by worshipful listening.

I love you because you are helping me to make of the lumber of my life not a tavern but a Temple, and of the words of my every day not a reproach but a song. I love you because you have done more than any creed could have done to make me good, and more than any fate could have done to make me happy. You have done it just by being yourself. Perhaps that is what being a friend means after all.

Love is a symbol of eternity. It wipes out all sense of time, destroying all memory of a beginning and all fear of an end.

ANNE-LOUISE-GERMAINE DE STAEL

They who love are but one step from heaven.

JAMES RUSSELL LOWELL

Love looks through a telescope; envy, through a microscope.

JOHN BILLINGS

In all the crowded universe
There is but one stupendous world: Love.
There is no tree that rears its crest,
No fern or flower that cleaves the sod,
Nor bird that sings above its nest,
But tries to speak this
word of God.

JOSIAH GILBERT HOLLAND

The Alabaster Box

Do not keep the alabaster box of your love and friendship sealed up until your friends are dead. Fill their lives with sweetness. Speak approving, cheering words while their ears can hear them, and while their hearts can be thrilled and made happier. The kind things you mean to say when they are gone, say before they go.

GEORGE W. CHILDS

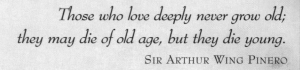

Those who love deeply never grow old;
they may die of old age, but they die young.

SIR ARTHUR WING PINERO

If we are to make a mature adjustment to life,
we must be able to give and receive love.

ANNA TREGO HUNTER

We are shaped and fashioned
by what we love.

JOHANN WOLFGANG
von GOETHE

In the triangle of love between ourselves, God, and other people, is found the secret of existence, and the best foretaste, I suspect, that we can have on earth of what heaven will probably be like.

SAMUEL M. SHOEMAKER

He who knows he is loved can be content with a piece of bread, while all the luxuries of the world cannot satisfy the craving of the lonely.

FRANCES J. ROBERTS

Love puts the fun in together…the sad in apart…
the hope in tomorrow…the joy in a heart.

Let love be purified, and all the rest will follow.
A pure love is thus, indeed, the panacea
for all the ills of the world.

HENRY DAVID THOREAU

Until I truly loved,
I was alone.

CAROLINE NORTON

You

Deep in the heart of me,
Nothing but You!
See through the art of me—
Deep in the heart of me
Find the best part of me,
Changeless and true.
Deep in the heart of me
Nothing but You!

RUTH GUTHRIE HARDING

Love, like a spring rain, is pretty hard to be in the middle of without getting some on you.

FRANK A. CLARK

Dear friends, let us love one another, for love comes from God. Everyone who loves has been born of God and knows God. Whoever does not love does not know God, because God is love.

1 JOHN 4:7,8

Love cannot be inactive; its life is a ceaseless effort to know, to feel, and to realize the boundless treasures hidden its depths. This is its insatiable desire.

JAN VAN RUYSBROECK

Alone and without love we die. Life itself is as dependent on relationship with others as it is on food.

M. N. BECK

Take away love and our earth is a tomb.

ROBERT BROWNING

Love and Live

To love abundantly is to live abundantly, and to love for ever
is to live for ever. Hence, eternal life is inextricably
bound up with love. We want to live for ever
for the same reason we want to live
tomorrow. Why do you want to
live tomorrow? It is because
there is someone who loves you,
and whom you want to

see tomorrow, and be with, and love back. There is no other reason why we should live on than that we love and are beloved. It is when a man has no one to love him that he commits suicide. So long as he has friends, those who love him and whom he loves, he will live; because to live is to love.

HENRY DRUMMOND

Of all earthly music that which reaches farthest into heaven is the beating of a truly loving heart.

HENRY WARD BEECHER

The Look of Love

What does love look like? It has hands to help others.
It has feet to hasten to the poor and needy.
It has eyes to see misery and want.
It has ears to hear the sighs
and sorrows of men.
That is what
love looks like.

AUGUSTINE

There is no way under the sun of making a man worthy of love, except by loving him.

THOMAS MERTON

To be able to say how much you love is to love little.

PETRARCH

Love is the medicine for the sickness of the world.

KARL AUGUSTUS MENNINGER

CHAPTER TWO
The Greatest of These

Everyone has asked himself the great question of antiquity as of the modern world: What is the summum bonum—the supreme good? You have life before you. Once only you can live it. What is the noblest object of desire, the supreme gift to covet?

We have been told that the greatest thing in the religious world is faith. That great word has been the keynote for centuries of the popular religion; and we have easily learned to look upon it as the greatest thing in the world. Well, we are wrong. If we have been told that, we may miss the mark.

In the thirteenth chapter of 1 Corinthians, Paul takes us to spiritual living at its source; and there we see, "The greatest of these is love."

It is not an oversight. Paul was speaking of faith just a moment before. He says, "If I have all faith, so that I can remove mountains, and have not love, I am nothing." So far from forgetting, he deliberately contrasts them, "Now abideth faith, hope, love," and without a moment's hesitation the decision falls, "the greatest of these is love."

And it is not prejudice. A man is apt to recommend to others his own strong point. The observing student can detect a beautiful tenderness growing and ripening all through his character as Paul gets old; but the hand that wrote, "The greatest of these is love," when we meet it first, is stained with blood.

Nor is this letter to the Corinthians peculiar in singling out love as the summum bonum. The masterpieces of scripture are agreed about it. Peter says, "Above all things have fervent love among yourselves." Above all things. And John goes farther, "God is love."

Thus we are left without any doubts. Love is the supreme good in life; love is the greatest of these.

HENRY DRUMMOND

CHAPTER THREE

Learning to Love

You learn to speak by speaking, to study by studying, to run by running, to work by working; and just so you learn to love God and man by loving. Begin as a mere apprentice, and the very power of love will lead you on to become a master of the art.

SAINT FRANCIS OF SALES

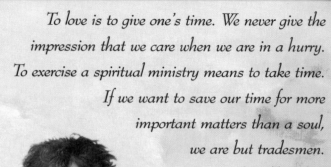

To love is to give one's time. We never give the impression that we care when we are in a hurry. To exercise a spiritual ministry means to take time. If we want to save our time for more important matters than a soul, we are but tradesmen.

PAUL TOURNIER

Love is the forgetting of oneself in the service of another.

R. AINSLEY BARNWELL

To love for the sake of being loved is human,
but to love for the sake of loving is angelic.

ALPHONSE DE LAMARTINE

Love is a decision
to serve someone.

DONALD E. WHITNEY

Love has a hem on its garment
that reaches the very dust;
It touches the dirt of the streets and lanes
And because it can, it must.

ANONYMOUS

The deepest truth blooms
only from the deepest love.

HEINRICH HEINE

They that love beyond the world cannot be separated.
Death cannot kill what never dies. Nor can spirits
ever be divided that love and live in the same divine
principle; the root and record of their friendship.
Death is but crossing the world,
as friends do the seas, they
live in one another still.

WILLIAM PENN

It is easy for them who have never been loved to sneer at love.

WELSH PROVERB

Love must be learned again and again; there is no end to it.
Hate needs no instruction, but waits only to be provoked.

KATHERINE ANNE PORTER

The love of our neighbor
is the only door out of
the dungeon of self.

GEORGE MACDONALD

Give It Away

Love is the one treasure that multiplies by division. It is the one gift that grows bigger the more you take from it. It is the one business in which it pays to be an absolute spendthrift. You can give it away, throw it away, empty your pockets, shake the basket, turn the glass upside down, and tomorrow you will have more than ever.

ANONYMOUS

Love must be sincere. Hate what is evil; cling to what is good. Be devoted to one another in brotherly love. Honor one another above yourselves.

ROMANS 12:9-10

We don't love qualities, we love a person; sometimes by reason of their defects as well as their qualities.

JACQUES MARITAIN

Hate cannot destroy hate, but love can and does.
Not the soft and negative thing that has carried
the name and misrepresented the emotion, but love
that suffers all things and is kind, love that
accepts responsibility, love that marches,
love that suffers, love that bleeds
and dies for a great cause —
but to rise again.

DANIEL A. POLING

Love does not parade the imperfections of others or taunt people for their weaknesses. Rather love seeks to understand others their imperfections and weaknesses.

ANONYMOUS

Love makes everything lovely; hate concentrates itself on the one thing hated.

GEORGE MACDONALD

When I have learnt to love God better than my
earthly dearest, I shall love my earthly
dearest better than I do now.

C. S. LEWIS

Love is something so divine,
Description would but make it less;
'Tis what I feel, but can't define,
'Tis what I know,
but can't express.

BEILBY PORTEUS

Nothing Sweeter

Nothing is sweeter than love, nothing stronger, nothing higher, nothing wider, nothing more pleasant, nothing fuller or better in heaven or on earth…A lover flies, runs, rejoices…Love often knows no limits but is fervent beyond measure. Love feels no burden, thinks nothing of labors, attempts what is above its strength, pleads no excuse of impossibility...Though wearied, it is not tired; though pressed, it is not straitened; though alarmed, it is not confounded; but as a lively flame and burning torch, it forces its way upwards and passes securely through all.

THOMAS Á KEMPIS

There is no greater love than the love that holds
on where there seems nothing
left to hold on to.

G.W.C. THOMAS

I am convinced that nine out of every ten persons seeing a psychiatrist do not need one. They need somebody who will love them with God's love...and they will get well.

PAUL TOURNIER

Love is the salt that savors the whole [of life] and drives away the mists so that the sun may eternally shine.

GEORGE MATTHEW ADAMS

The Only Thing

There's only one thing in this world that's worth having.
Love. L-o-v-e. You love somebody, somebody loves you.
That's all there is to it. But if you don't get that,
you've got nothing. So you take the next best thing.
You take power or money or fame or whatever
little morsel you can pick up for
yourself as second best.

CHARLES MERGENDAHL

Love isn't like a reservoir. You'll never drain it dry. It's much more like a natural spring. The longer and the farther it flows, the stronger and the deeper and the clearer it becomes.

EDDIE CANTOR

He is all fault who hath no fault at all. For who loves me must have a touch of earth.

ALFRED, LORD TENNYSON

We are all born for love. It is the
principle of existence, and its only end.

BENJAMIN DISRAELI

Love is never lost.
If not reciprocated it will
flow back and soften and
purify the heart.

WASHINGTON IRVING

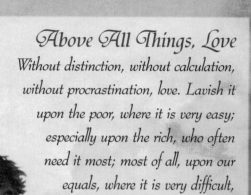

Above All Things, Love

Without distinction, without calculation,
without procrastination, love. Lavish it
upon the poor, where it is very easy;
especially upon the rich, who often
need it most; most of all, upon our
equals, where it is very difficult,
and for whom perhaps
we each do least of all.

HENRY DRUMMOND

CHAPTER FOUR
Born to Love

We all need love. With all our complexities, we are not easy creatures to satisfy. We cannot meet the conditions of a satisfied life by gorging ourselves, lying down on the grass, and staring at the clouds. We have deeper needs than the brute, and the deepest one is love.

Babies cannot live on milk alone. They are born with a nature that requires love. There are many confirmed cases in which babies who received nourishment and shelter wasted away for a lack of love. With the passing of time the once baby-now-adult has a greater need to give love than to receive it, to feel love more than he needs to be felt by it.

But we often think too much in terms of receiving love instead of giving it. However, we are not babies and as adults we need to scatter our affections around. We grownups like attention, too. We enjoy being pampered. It is gratifying to receive. But there is much more fulfillment and higher ecstasy in having a heart so filled with love that it finds more joy in giving than in receiving.

Our need for love is born within us. Without the ministries of love we would perish. The child is born with a greater need to receive love than to give it; yet as he develops, the need becomes urgent in both respects.

The need of love is as universal as man himself. Wherever we walk, on every shore and in every clime, the need of love walks by our side. Our hearts cry out for affection. This implanted longing is proof that we are akin to God for "God is love."

As the child receives love it learns to give love. That beginning emotion normally grows and grows until it embraces many people, even self, and many things. As this lovely force multiplies, it contributes to the spark and vigor of the individual, preparing him for a life a little lower than the angels. It is so essential and marvelous that Friedrich Von Schiller, in an appreciative and inquisitive mood, asked: "What is life without the radiance of love?"

Love is not fantasy. It is not just a topic for poets and philosophers. It is not just an idealistic longing for those who roam the silvery heavens. It is a state of the heart for *now* and *here*, for the people on earth. Loving is as real as living. It is the power we need to traverse life's pathway and to hurdle the obstacles. It is the cushion that softens the hard knocks we receive; it is the consideration that pillows the gentle blows we give.

Love controls conduct. No mad dog has it. And when a world turns mad, it is devoid of it.

It is not trite, therefore, to say that love will solve our problems, no more stereotyped than to say that food sustains life. Without food we die, and without love we die a death worse than physical. Let's keep our values in their true perspective and not depreciate them because the need has always existed. Let's rather mark up their value and live, live as exalted creatures on the high summit of tender attachment which many have not yet attained.

LEROY BROWNLOW

CHAPTER FIVE

The Measure of Love

We never know how much one loves till we know how much he is willing to endure and suffer for us; and it is the suffering element that measures love. The characters that are great must, of necessity, be characters that shall be willing, patient and strong to endure for others.

To hold our nature in the willing service of another,
is the divine idea of manhood,
of the human character.
HENRY WARD BEECHER

Human things must be known to be loved:
but Divine things must be
loved to be known.
BLAISE PASCAL

One of the great illusions of our time is that love is self-sustaining. It is not. Love must be fed and nurtured, constantly renewed. That demands ingenuity and consideration, but first and foremost, it demands time.

DAVID R. MACE

If we spend our lives in loving,
we have no leisure to complain,
or to feel unhappiness.

JOSEPH JOUBERT

The Flavors of Love

Joy is love exalted; peace is love in repose; long-suffering is love enduring; gentleness is love in society; goodness is love in action; faith is love on the battlefield; meekness is love in school; and temperance is love in training.

DWIGHT LYMAN MOODY

Loving, like prayer, is a power as well as a process. It's curative. It is creative.

ZONA GALE

May the Lord make your love increase and overflow for each
other and for everyone else, just as ours does for you.

1 Thessalonians 3:12

In real love you want the other person's good.
In romantic love you want the other person.

Margaret Anderson

Fulfillment in life comes not by
the love of power but by
the power of love.

Love is not a possession but a growth. The heart is a lamp with just oil enough to burn for an hour, and if there be no oil to put in again its light will go out. God's grace is the oil that fills the lamp of love.

HENRY WARD BEECHER

Duty does not have to be dull.
Love can make it beautiful
and fill it with life.

THOMAS MERTON

Tell me how much you know of the suffering of your fellow men, and I will tell you how much you have loved them.

HELMUT THIELICKE

A wise lover values not so much the gift of the lover as the love of the giver.

THOMAS À KEMPIS

Love Can

I never knew a night so black
Light failed to follow in its track.

I never knew a storm so gray
It failed to have its clearing day.

I never knew such bleak despair
That there was not a rift somewhere.

I never knew an hour so drear
Love could not fill it full of cheer.

JOHN KENDRICK BANGS

Love is giving freely, expecting nothing in return.
Law concerns itself with an equitable exchange,
this for that. Law is made necessary by people;
love is made possible by God.

MARY CARSON

You can give without loving,
but cannot love
without giving.

AMY CARMICHAEL

It is not the most lovable individuals who stand more in need of love, but the most unlovable.

<small>ASHLEY MONTAGU</small>

Holding a beggar's child
Against my heart,
Through blinding tears I see
That as I love the tiny, piteous thing,
So God loves me!

<small>TOYOCHIKO KAGAWA</small>

Love is like a friendship caught on fire. In the beginning a flame, very pretty, often hot and fierce but still only light and flickering. As love grows older, our hearts mature and our love becomes as coals, deep-burning and unquenchable.

BRUCE LEE

Love cures people—both the ones who give it and the ones who receive it.

KARL AUGUSTUS MENNINGER

When you know that God loves you, it helps you love yourself.
And when you love yourself, you can love somebody else.

KARI MILTON

Love alone is capable of uniting living beings in such a way
as to complete and fulfill them, for it alone takes them
and joins them by what is
deepest in themselves.

PIERRE TEILHARD DE CHARDIN

At Journey's End

Mortals, while through the world you go,
Hope may succor and faith befriend,
Yet happy your hearts if you can but know,
Love awaits at the journey's end!

CLINTON SCOLLARD

Love is difficult to sustain, not because it is a positive emotion, but because it is a complex one. Hate is easy to maintain for a lifetime because it is a simple one. Love might be compared to the building of a tall and elaborate sandcastle, taking many hours of painstaking effort, cooperation, balance, and persistence; and hate might be compared to the foot that comes along and with one vicious or thoughtless kick destroys in a moment what has been built up.

SYDNEY J. HARRIS

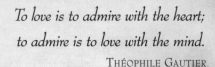

To love is to admire with the heart;
to admire is to love with the mind.

THÉOPHILE GAUTIER

No cord or cable can draw so forcibly, or bind so fast,
as love can do with a single thread.

ROBERT BURTON

Wheresoever a man seeketh his own,
there he falleth from love.

THOMAS Á KEMPIS

Instead of allowing yourself to be so unhappy, just let your love grow as God wants it to grow; seek goodness in others, love more persons more; love them more impersonally, more unselfishly, without thought of return. The return, never fear, will take care of itself.

HENRY DRUMMOND

To love anyone is nothing else than to wish that person good.

ST. THOMAS AQUINAS

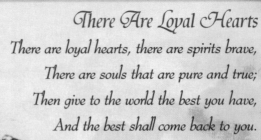

There Are Loyal Hearts

There are loyal hearts, there are spirits brave,

There are souls that are pure and true;

Then give to the world the best you have,

And the best shall come back to you.

Give love, and love to your

heart will flow, a strength

in your utmost need;

Have faith, and a score

of hearts will show.

Their faith in your word and deed.

For life is the mirror of king and slave.

'Tis just what you are and do;

Then give to the world the best you have,

And the best will come back to you.

MADELINE BRIDGE

Love is a tender plant; when properly nourished, it becomes
sturdy and enduring, but neglected it will soon wither and die.

HUGH B. BROWN

The norm or measure by which any thought or action is
to be judged a success or failure,
right or wrong, is love.

JOSEPH FLETCHER

Life is the flower of which
love is the honey.

VICTOR HUGO

CHAPTER SIX
Love Is Forever

Seas have their source,
and so have shallow springs;
and love is love, in beggars as in kings.

SIR EDWARD DYER

Love is available to all. That lets each speak love in his own way and live it in the bounds of his own practicality. That permits each to demonstrate it, and that is the prettiest poetry and the grandest elocution.

Love is simple. The centuries have passed. The profoundest philosophers have walked on platform and spoken. The most accomplished poets have taken pen and written. But no human being has ever put together a stronger statement on love than the simple expression, "I love you." This is heart language.

The most satisfying joy in all the world is in having a person dearer to you than your own self, a person with whom you feel free to pour out and share your every thought, your every grief and your every joy; for it is with that person you feel a deep unity of spirits. This is love. For:

Love alone is capable of uniting living beings in such a way as to complete and fulfill them, for it alone takes them and joins them by what is deepest in themselves.

PIERRE TEILHARD DE CHARDIN

What inspiration, what strength, what buoyancy it gives to know that if all the rest of the world should turn against you, rend you and forsake you, there is one person who will never wrong you by an unjust thought or unkind word or unmerciful deed, one person who will cling to you in poverty and in persecution, in disaster and in death, one person who will sacrifice all things for you and for whom you will sacrifice all things, even life. This person's welfare is your greatest concern. And it is with this person you expect never to be separated except by death. This is companionate love.

Maturity is one of the chief traits of love. Learning to love is an act of maturity. When love matures, so does the person. In Paul's brilliant and splendorous description of love, he explains:

When I was a child, I talked like a child,
I thought like a child, I reasoned like a child.
When I became a man, I put childish ways behind me.

1 CORINTHIANS 13:11

As we become more grown in love we outgrow our immaturity. We say the individual is a big, big person, and he is; he is too big to whimper, complain, nettle, find fault, or forever feel mistreated. His maturity lets him reach out of self and identify with another, and thus bear and share with the other person. Maturity enables us to stand in the other fellow's shoes, as it were, and to walk in them and limp because of the pebble which the intolerant never notice. The mature feel with others while the immature only ache with their own needs.

The richer the personality, the easier it is for love to compound itself, even increasing in delight and satisfaction with every enlargement. This is natural, for love, the embodiment of all that is good and pure, lives on love.

Whatever love we have and it does come in degrees feed it and it will grow, and as it expands so will our personality.

But with some, love is more difficult. The reason is that their concept of love was distorted in childhood, and today they have a false image of love. They may see it as something selfish and demanding, cruel and domineering, an inconsistent way of life more concerned with itself than with the one they love. Of course, they experienced only a distortion of professed love. As a result, these people now in adulthood meet love with resentment. For all have a tendency to pull away from unpleasant experiences.

The people who are scared of love rebound against it. This is why some rebel at love and start hating anyone who loves them, though they may not be fully conscious of it.

The normal pattern is expressed in the Bible, a super book on psychology, in a more reciprocal reaction: "We love him, because he first loved us" (1 John 4:19). This is the normal response to love.

So when a person finds it hard to love, perhaps something went awry in his development. The true self was stepped on. The fuller life of love was checked. But this condition is not hopeless. Nothing is hopeless with us for the simple reason we are human, we have intelligence, will and a soul, which enable us to replace selfishness with big-heartedness and hate with love.

For us to love others properly we must first love ourselves rightly. Of course, the correct balance must be kept. In correcting an imbalance, it is unfortunate that love for self has been attacked when it is actually a virtue essential to self-preservation. It is only a perversion of loving self that is the culprit. The Second Commandment of the law is based on self-love: "Love your neighbor as yourself" (Matthew 22:39). This is proof that self-love when linked with a love for others is not evil.

LEROY BROWNLOW

CHAPTER SEVEN
Loving Hearts

Many waters cannot quench love, neither can the floods drown it.

SONG OF SOLOMON 8:7

One loving heart sets another on fire.

AUGUSTINE

*Where love is not,
there can be no pleasures.*

RUSSIAN PROVERB

Love and Sunshine

You are as prone to love as the sun is to shine; it being the most delightful and natural employment of the Soul of Man: without which you are dark and miserable. For certainly he that delights not in Love makes vain the universe, and is of necessity to himself the greatest burden.

THOMAS TRAHERNE

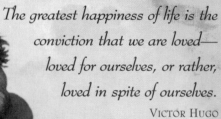

Whatever a man loves, that is his god. For he carries it in his heart; he goes about it night and day; he sleeps and wakes with it, be it what it may—wealth or self, pleasure or renown.

MARTIN LUTHER

The greatest happiness of life is the conviction that we are loved— loved for ourselves, or rather, loved in spite of ourselves.

VICTOR HUGO

By the accident of fortune a man may rule the world for a time, but by virtue of love he may rule the world forever.

LAO-TZE

Dear children, let us not love with words or tongue but with actions and in truth.

1 JOHN 3:18

Love slays what we have been that we may be what we were not.

AUGUSTINE

There can be no peace on earth until we have learned to respect the dignity of man and are willing to build on the foundation of human love the kind of world that the great teachers of mankind have portrayed to us from the time of the Ten Commandments and the Sermon on the Mount. These are the true lessons of mortal life.

DAVID LAWRENCE

O Brother Man, fold to thy heart thy brother;
Where pity dwells, the peace of God is there;
To worship rightly is to love each other,
Each smile a hymn, each kindly deed a prayer.

JOHN GREENLEAF WHITTIER

Whoever lives true life will love true love.

ELIZABETH BARRETT BROWNING

Love is the key to the universe which unlocks all doors.

ANONYMOUS

He that falls in love with himself will have no rivals.

BENJAMIN FRANKLIN

If your love be pure, simple, and well ordered,
you shall be free from bondage.

THOMAS Á KEMPIS

Love gives itself; it is not bought.

HENRY WADSWORTH LONGFELLOW

The Power of Love

Love is the greatest constraining power in the world. Tell me what you love, and I will tell you what you are. The man who loves needs no law to impel him to action. This works on both sides of the moral line. The man who loves right and righteousness will do right, law or no law, while the man who loves wrong will do wrong in spite of all law.

ANONYMOUS

So long as we love, we serve. So long as we are loved
by others, I would almost say we are indispensable;
and no man is useless while he has a friend.

ROBERT LOUIS STEVENSON

Forgetting oneself is not
a refinement of love. It is
a first condition of love.

LEON JOSEPH SUENENS

Our Lord does not care so much for the importance of our works as for the love with which they are done.

TERESA OF AVILA

Love comforteth like sunshine after rain.

WILLIAM SHAKESPEARE

Love is the only service that power cannot command and money cannot buy.

ANONYMOUS

Love is the weapon which Omnipotence reserved to conquer rebel man when all the rest had failed. Reason he parries; fear he answers blow for blow; future interest he meets with present pleasure; but love is that sun against whose melting beams the winter cannot stand. There is not one human being in a million, nor a thousand men in all earth's huge quintillion whose clay heart is hardened against love.

MARTIN FARQUHAR TUPPER

The way to love anything is to realize that it might be lost.

G. K. Chesterton

But the fruit of the Spirit is love, joy, peace, patience, kindness, goodness, faithfulness, gentleness and self-control.

Galatians 5:22

There is no remedy for love
but to love more.

Henry David Thoreau

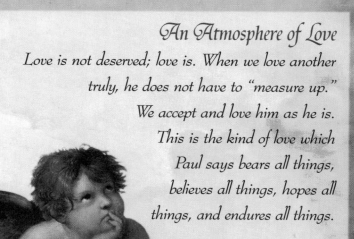

An Atmosphere of Love

Love is not deserved; love is. When we love another truly, he does not have to "measure up." We accept and love him as he is. This is the kind of love which Paul says bears all things, believes all things, hopes all things, and endures all things.

When we know that we are loved in this way,
then and only then, can we dare throw our masks
into the corner and reveal ourselves. Only in
such an atmosphere of love and acceptance
can real trust, intimacy, and openness
flourish and grow.

WYNNE GILLIS

Love expects without expecting too much. Love looks for a return in kind without automatically demanding it. Love focuses on a present relationship while moving forward toward a future goal. Love believes with God in a new day.

WILLIAM HIEMSTRA

Love has power to give in a moment what toil can scarcely reach in an age.

JOHANN WOLFGANG VON GOETHE

Most men need more love than they deserve.

MARIE VON EBNER-ESCHENBACH

Miracles

The cure for all the ills and wrongs, the cares, the sorrows, and the crimes of humanity, all lie in that one word "love." It is the divine vitality that everywhere produces and restores life. To each and every one of us, it gives the power of working miracles if we will.

LYDIA MARIA CHILD